ARTEM KUDELIA PHD

Drama Therapy

Potential of Psychodrama and Family Constellations

First edition

ISBN (paperback): 9798853586291
ISBN (hardcover): 9798853586307

This book was professionally typeset on Reedsy.
Find out more at reedsy.com

Contents

Acknowledgments

I would like to express my gratitude to my psychology and psychotherapy teachers, who have opened the path and laid a solid foundation of knowledge. Furthermore, I extend my immense appreciation to patients, colleagues, friends, and all individuals who directly or indirectly contributed to the writing of this book.

BONUS: Get Your Free Resources Now

I'm excited to share a **free eBook** and **exclusive access** to **psychological resources** with you. To get started, scan the QR code or visit psychemaster.com/drama-therapy

What You'll Get:

- **Free eBook**: Explore advanced psychotherapeutic techniques and approaches that complement the insights.
- **Interactive Learning**: Engage with exercises and quizzes to solidify your understanding of complex theories.
- **Latest Research**: Stay updated with the most recent findings in the field of psychotherapy and integrative therapy approaches.
- **Continuous Support**: Get consistent tips, strategies, and motivation to assist you in staying focused and excelling in your studies and practice.

Maximize your understanding of psychotherapy!

Jacob Moreno and Psychodrama

The creator of dramatic psychotherapeutic work is Jacob Moreno, a Romanian psychologist, psychiatrist, and sociologist. He is often credited as the pioneer of group psychotherapy, as no other psychiatrists conducted therapeutic activities for groups of patients or published articles on this topic prior to him.

Moreno was born in Bucharest in 1889 to a Sephardic Jewish family from the Ottoman Empire. In 1895, his family moved to Vienna, where he remained after his parents' subsequent move to Berlin in 1905.

Jacob Moreno

Moreno describes a particular mystical experience that occurred when he was 14 years old while standing in front of a statue of Christ in a German town. He writes, "Standing before the statue, I began to understand that I had to make a decision that would determine my entire future. I believe that all people make such a decision in their youth. And then my moment came. I was faced with the question of what I should choose as mine: the entire universe or my family, the lineage from which I came? And I chose the universe—not because my family was worse than other families, but because I wanted to live for something greater, for the world to which every member of my family belongs and where I would like to see them return. My decision meant that all people are my brothers and sisters; all mothers and fathers are my mothers and fathers; all children, regardless of their parents, are my children; and all women are my wives. All the property in this world is my property, and, conversely, everything I have belongs to the whole world."

This experience, apparently, became one of the philosophical foundations of his psychotherapy method and contributed to the formation of the belief that "true psychotherapy can only be the psychotherapy of all humanity."

In 1909, he enrolled at the University of Vienna, where he studied philosophy and medicine.

Moreno writes that in 1912, he met Sigmund Freud only once when, while working at a psychiatric clinic, he attended Freud's lecture on the analysis of telepathic dreams. Moreno and Freud struck up a conversation, and Freud asked Moreno what he was involved in. Moreno replied, "Well, Dr. Freud, I start where you stop. You meet people in an artificial office setting, while I meet them on the street or at their homes in their natural environment. You analyze their dreams, but I try to give them the courage to dream. I teach people how to play God." Moreno noted that Freud looked at him incomprehensibly after his vivid metaphor.

During his education, he decided to pursue a career in psychiatry. In 1913, he began his first psychotherapeutic experiments in collaboration with the physician S. Gruen and the journalist K. Kalber. They created small psychotherapeutic groups for girls, consisting of 8 to 10 participants. The groups met two to three times a week to discuss various problematic situations that arose in their lives.

In 1915–1916, Moreno worked in a refugee camp in Mitten-wald, Austria. During this work, he gained an important creative insight that would eventually lead him to the development of sociometry. He discovered that if people were distributed in the barracks according to their race, religion, and political views, it could significantly improve their emotional state and quality of life.

In 1917, he graduated from medical school and became a

physician. Moreno writes, "Psychodrama came into being on the 'fool's day,' April 1, 1921, between 7 and 10 in the evening."It was in 1921 that Jacob Levy Moreno began regularly applying his method to address various emotional and behavioral problems. A case described in the history of psychodrama is considered a significant turning point. It involved a man who had decided to end his life through suicide. Working together with his friend Mariana Lornitzo, Moreno decided to conduct a psychodramatic enactment with the man, in which they acted out his fantasies. This work prevented the suicide and further solidified Moreno's belief in the effectiveness of his chosen course of psychotherapeutic work.

Another notable case in the development of psychodrama as a psychotherapeutic method was the "Barbara case," which took place in 1922. Barbara was an actress who often played innocent girls in her theatrical performances. However, when she was alone, she transformed into a true fury, attacking her husband George with her fists and using foul language. Moreno suggested that she play the role of a dirty prostitute in his therapeutic theater who would have a scandal with her pimp and eventually be killed by him. After this enactment, Barbara experienced some changes. Something that wanted to emerge from within her outside of the theater found its place. In subsequent enactments, she occasionally played similar roles as scandalous women, noting that each role helped balance something within her. Another focus of attention became the joint enactment of their domestic quarrels with her husband.

Moreno writes about this: "After a few months, Barbara, George, and I sat together in the theater. They rediscovered themselves and each other, or rather, they discovered themselves and each other for the first time. I analyzed the course of

4

their psychodrama session after session and explained to them how their healing occurred."

There is a popular legend about Moreno and his childhood when he climbed into the basement with a group of neighborhood boys and suggested they play God. It is worth noting that this is a highly peculiar game for young children. Jacob told the others that he would be God, and they would be his angels. The children agreed and constructed "heavens" for him using whatever materials were available. Jacob sat on them, and the other children, acting as angels, ran around him and sang various songs. One boy asked Jacob why he couldn't fly. To meet his comrade's expectations, Jacob attempted to "fly" but ended up falling and breaking his arm. In the future, Moreno will comment on this experience as his first attempt at working with the psychodrama method, jokingly calling it the "therapy of fallen gods."

In 1924, Moreno published a book titled "The Theater of Spontaneity," in which he identified four different types of theater.

1. **Theater of Conflict**: In this theater, conflicts are resolved at the psychological level.
2. **Improvisational Theater**: This level reveals the creative potential of the individual.
3. **Therapeutic Theater**: In this theater, a person plays themselves.
4. **Theater of Creation**: This theater allows individuals to grow and self-actualize.

In 1925, after the death of his father and his arrival in the United States, Jacob took his father's name as his surname and became known to the world as Jacob Levy Moreno. It is also worth noting that in the Hebrew language, the word "Morenu" means "teacher," so there may be several reasons for the name change.

In 1931, Moreno embarked on a research study in Sing Sing prison, where he applied his sociometry as the primary method of investigation. Afterwards, when the work was completed, he presented the research findings at a meeting of the American Psychiatric Association, where he proposed his vision for creating a healthier prison community. It is reported that it was during this meeting that Moreno publicly used the term "group psychotherapy" for the first time.

In 1934, he published his main book on sociometry, "Who Shall Survive?"

In 1936, he established his own psychiatric clinic, "Beacon Hill," which became the source of psychodrama's dissemination worldwide.

In 1937, he began publishing the journal "Sociometry: Journal of Interpersonal Relations."

In 1946, the first volume of his book "Psychodrama" was released.

Starting in 1950, Moreno began traveling to many countries, spreading his method. Through Moreno's work and the efforts of his students, who also disseminated the method in other countries upon his request, psychodrama gained global recognition and application.

In 1974, Moreno passed away.

Jacob Moreno expressed intriguing philosophical thoughts about the idea that the divine act of creation is not complete but continues here and now. He believed that individuals can serve as conduits for the creative work of God through spontaneity in the "here and now" state. Moreno also believed that it is through the manifestation of spontaneity that individuals can "encounter" God. Moreno offers his definition of spontaneity as an adequate response to new conditions or a new response to old conditions. His philosophy is imbued with divine metaphors that he skillfully employs, thus establishing a certain foundation for his method.

In his works, Moreno describes three types of spontaneity in communication:

1. **Transference**: This term, in Moreno's understanding, carries the same meaning as in the theories of Sigmund Freud. It refers to the transfer of one's own feelings and beliefs onto another person.
2. **Empathy**: This manifestation of spontaneity involves refraining from judgments and assumptions and objectively sensing another person as they are.
3. **Tele**: The participation of all communication partners as active subjects in the interaction. It entails mutual acceptance of roles.

A significant part of the psychodramatic method is Moreno's sociometry. Its philosophy states that any person, upon entering a social context, gradually forms a specific matrix of meanings concerning the characteristics of the people around them. Some individuals are perceived more as potential friends; others evoke sexual preferences, and still, others create the impression of people with whom one can interact excellently in a business context. Each such characteristic can be evaluated based on the level of its intensity. A sociometric test can provide invaluable information for understanding the functioning of a group and how to reorganize it to achieve any necessary

7

qualitative changes within it.

One of the key concepts in psychodrama is "role-playing," in which participants portray and explore various facets of emotions and behaviors. Unlike conventional theater, role-playing in psychodrama is not something rehearsed or pre-planned; instead, it arises from the actor's own spontaneity and manifestations.

According to Moreno, the ultimate product of spontaneity is "cultural conserves," which are elements that contribute to the preservation of cultural traditions: language, art, literature, rituals, and so on. In other words, everything that creates a connection with past experiences while also addressing challenges that may arise in the future.

In psychodrama therapy, the term "catharsis" is used, which originated in ancient Greece and meant "an emotionally cleansing experience." The various strong emotions expressed during the process of role-playing possess precisely such a quality and can lead to significant changes in both the cognitive and behavioral domains for the individuals directly expressing them and for those observing the role-playing process.

The facilitator of psychodramatic theater, following theatrical tradition, is referred to as the director and assumes three roles during the process.

1. **Producer**: The performer in this role guides the staging process, fulfills an organizational function, and helps actualize specific elements of the work into reality.
2. **Therapist**: This role assists the patient in working through specific behavioral and emotional patterns and provides necessary support.
3. **Analyst**: The function of this role is the interpretation

and analysis of the participants' behavior within the group process. Rational understanding is also a significant part of the psychodramatic therapy process.

The group member who assumes the central role is called the protagonist. Formally, the patient with whom the therapist works is the protagonist in the dramatic play process. However, it is possible for other participants to take on the protagonist's role if the need arises. Participants who play various other roles during the process are referred to as "auxiliary egos." The audience consists of other group members who are not directly involved in the ongoing psychodramatic enactment.

In psychodrama, there are specific phases of the therapy process. The following are distinguished:

1. **Warm-up**: It can be verbal or non-verbal. During this phase, various participants' concerns and themes are explored. A warm-up can also be useful for individuals who may still exhibit resistance to fully engaging in the psychodramatic play.

2. **Psychodramatic action**: This refers to the actual portrayal on stage, which may be chosen by the director based on their own understanding of the necessity and appropriateness of a particular element of the actors' performance. However, the patient themselves can also make choices and propose specific scenes for enactment.

3. **Subsequent discussion**: After the psychodramatic action itself, the protagonist and other group members have the opportunity to share the peculiarities of their emotional experiences with each other. Such discussions contribute to the integration of acquired experiences at a deeper

personal level.

It should be noted that specific methodologies are employed in the psychodramatic process that facilitate participants' self-expression and are integral to the therapeutic process. Let us enumerate some of them.

1. **Monologue**: In a monologue, the protagonist freely expresses their feelings through lines of dialogue. This allows for a deeper awareness of their internal psychological processes through controlled self-expression.

2. **Doubling**: In this practice, another group member begins to mirror the verbal and non-verbal reactions of the protagonist, thereby supporting them and helping them better comprehend their thoughts, emotions, and behavioral responses.

3. **Role reversal**: This practice enables the protagonist to assume a secondary role in the psychodramatic session while another person who previously played the role of an "auxiliary ego" takes on the protagonist's original role. This process can contribute to a more multifaceted understanding of the context and provide an opportunity to see the situation from different perspectives.

4. **Reflection**: This practice is a variation of role reversal. In this case, another person takes on the role of the protagonist and portrays it. The actual protagonist observes the performance of their own role from an outsider's perspective.

Jacob Moreno writes about his understanding of the conscious and unconscious mind: "For the continually creating mind, there would be no division between the conscious and unconscious. The creator is like a runner, for whom the part of the road already run and the upcoming part qualitatively form a unified whole."

Therefore, in the psychology of the creative act, there is no division between the conscious and the unconscious.

Moreno is a great admirer of describing various concrete processes in the psyche using metaphorical language, often with a considerable degree of pathos. As a result, many of his notions about elementary mental processes may be in stark confrontation with the views of other psychologists and psychiatrists.

In his works, Moreno attempts to demonstrate that Stanislavski's works and his method, which postulate key principles of how actors can effectively immerse themselves in a role and perform within it, have no relevance to his ideas about spontaneity. Moreno believes that Stanislavski "reduces the factor of spontaneity to reactivating memories laden with affect. This approach associates improvisation with past experience rather than the present moment."

In this case, we clearly see that Moreno imparts meaning to his notions of spontaneity that separate them from an individual's past experience. From a philosophical standpoint, such a judgment may have value. However, when we discuss the neurophysiology of the brain and the manifestation of spontaneity in a person's personality, we discover that any spontaneous act cannot be detached from an individual's past experience and is generated based on it, or more accurately, through its prism.

In the end, Moreno goes so far as to call Freud and Stanislavski "colleagues," despite their work in different fields. He attributes them collegiality based on their orientation in their activities toward past experience.

Moreno writes about a specific body training that an actor can undergo to achieve relaxation and release their reflexive systems. He discusses specific gymnastic and dance exercises that can cultivate and shape a sense of spontaneity. He also writes about the unresolved issue for actors in the creative process, namely the problem of coordinating the verbal and the physical, as well as excluding from the role performance those actions and gestures that are not directly related to the psychodramatic process.

Virginia Satir and "Family Sculpture"

One of the most popular forms of dramatic work in psychother-apy is Virginia Satir's family therapy. She was born in 1916 on a farm in Wisconsin, USA. At the age of three, she had already learned to read, and by the age of nine, she had read all the books in her school library. She was the oldest of five children in her family.

In her childhood, Virginia often witnessed arguments between her parents, which caused her a great deal of suffering. When she was five years old, she had an appendectomy and had to spend several months in the hospital. It was during this time that her parents were going through a serious conflict and considering divorce. It was then that young Virginia exclaimed that she wanted to be the "judge over her parents." This experience likely influenced her future professional orientation and focus on reconciling various conflicts within patients' families.

Since 1927, Satir has been living in Milwaukee, Wisconsin. She strives to attend as many courses as possible to finish school quickly. She received her high school diploma in 1932 and entered the State Teachers College in Milwaukee. She earned a bachelor's degree in education and then worked as a teacher for several years. She wrote her thesis for a master's degree in psychology in 1943 but defended it only in 1948.

After graduating from university, she began an active psychotherapeutic practice. In the process of working with patients, she started to form her views on the psychotherapeutic process, focusing her attention on the fact that one patient's problems are inseparable from the problems of other family members. Therefore, it is necessary to work with the family as a whole to achieve the desired psychotherapeutic outcomes.

Virginia Satir

In 1955, Virginia worked at a psychiatric institute in Illinois. In her work, she endeavored to spread her philosophy of family focus among her colleagues.

In 1959, she participated in the creation of a research institute in Palo Alto, where she worked until 1966.

In 1962, Virginia received a grant from the NIMH, which allowed her to organize the first training program in family psychotherapy. This is why she is often called the "mother of family psychotherapy."

In 1964, she published her first book, "Conjoint Family Therapy," based on a textbook she wrote for students.

In 1973, Virginia Satir became a professor at the University of Wisconsin and the University of Chicago.

During the period from 1970 to 1980, her work was significantly influenced by the development of neuro-linguistic programming. John Grinder and Richard Bandler considered her one of the founders of NLP. Leslie Cameron-Bandler and Frank Pucelik became her notable students in this form of psychotherapeutic practice.

In 1984, Virginia called on family psychotherapists to shift the focus to nurturing relationships.

In 1987, she visited the USSR.

Satir was married twice but did not have children. Due to a failed pregnancy and its termination, she was unable to become a mother. Later, she adopted two girls. Regarding her unsuccessful family life, Virginia wrote, "I often thought, could I do what I do if I were married? And I realized, No! That's probably my destiny—to travel the world, helping people. Other people have a different fate."

Virginia Satir passed away in 1988.

In 1991, one of the students of John Grinder and Richard Bandler, Steve Andreas, wrote a book dedicated to Virginia Satir's practice. The book was titled "Patterns of Her Magic," in which he summarized the main patterns of her psychotherapeutic practice.

It is worth noting an interesting fact: according to two national American surveys of psychiatrists, psychologists, and social workers, Virginia Satir was recognized as one of the most influential psychotherapists.

Satir's work was permeated with the principles of humanism

and humanity. In her work, she constantly strived to sow the seeds of hope. She said, "The family is a microcosm. Knowing how to heal the family, I know how to heal the whole world."

During her therapeutic activities, she often used various group forms of meditation aimed at facilitating necessary therapeutic changes. One of her most famous meditative texts is "I Am Me."

Let's present the text of this meditation:

"I am me. There is no one else in the world like me. Everything that comes from me is genuinely mine. I own everything that is within me. My body, my feelings, my mouth, my voice, all my actions—both for others and for myself. My fantasies, my dreams, my hopes, and my fears all belong to me. All my triumphs and successes, all my failures and mistakes. Since I possess everything within myself, I can understand myself and be friends with myself in all my parts. I know that there are aspects of me that puzzle me and many others that I do not yet know. But as long as I am friendly and loving, I can confidently and hopefully seek solutions to the puzzles and ways to find out more about myself—no matter how I appear or sound, no matter what I say or do. And everything I think and feel at this moment is genuinely me. If later some parts of how I looked, sounded, thought, and felt turn out to be unfitting, I can discard that which is unfitting, keep the rest, and invent something new for that which I discarded. I can see, hear, feel, think, and speak. I have all the tools I need to survive, to be close to others, to be productive, and to find meaning and order in the world of people and things. I own myself, and therefore, I can design myself. I am me, and I am okay."

Virginia Satir proposed a model that classifies individuals based on the stereotypicality of their reactions to stressful conditions. She identified four personal profiles.

1. **Blamer:** If a person belongs to this profile, when faced with a situation they cannot solve or simply a situation that creates significant emotional tension for them, they start displaying strong aggressive emotions towards their surroundings. They begin to shout, accuse, demand, threaten, and so on. Responsibility is often shifted to others.

2. **Mourner:** It is the diametrical opposite of the "blamer." Any stressful, unclear, or threatening situation leads to tears, sobbing, lamenting, and harsh self-blame. They usually take all the blame for the situation upon themselves.

3. **Computer:** This profile avoids strong emotions, carefully restraining and controlling them. They make extensive use of intellectual jargon. The primary reaction to stress is moralizing, lecturing other people about their various actions, citing scientific statistics and other research that can validate the "computer's" righteousness.

4. **Distractor:** A person with this profile constantly redirects their attention to something insignificant and of little importance in stressful situations. The most common emotional reactions are surprise, confusion, and incomprehension. Actions become confused and inconsistent, which, in the overwhelming majority of cases, does not contribute to problem resolution.

Subsequently, Virginia Satir added another profile named the "**Balancer**." According to the author, individuals with this profile do not exhibit stereotypical reactions like representatives of other profiles. Their actions are constructive and purposeful. Strong emotional reactions are under the volitional control of the individual.

It is important to emphasize that the aforementioned behavioral reactions, characteristic of specific profiles, are activated and intensified specifically in the context of stress and are not simply habitual forms of behavior in society.

As the primary approach to solving family problems, Virginia Satir used a dramatic group form of interaction. In this process, she acted out specific conflict situations that arise within a family and, through restructuring the dramatic session, directed the therapeutic context in the necessary direction. She named this form of therapeutic dramatization "family sculpting" or "family reconstruction." According to Satir, the process itself creates a systemic understanding for patients of the behavioral and emotional processes occurring within the family context.

The technique of "family sculpting" allows for the physical organization of the symbolism of relationships within the family system. Each family member, in the process of therapeutic drama work, can create their own living family portrait by placing their relatives or the people who play their roles in a particular way. The experience of each family member finds its expression in the holistic dramatic picture. When family members witness the structure of communication within the family system, they gain a unique experience of awareness, which can lead to significant changes at the emotional and behavioral levels.

"Sculpting" is not only a means of transforming and changing the family system but also an excellent way to diagnose the characteristics of family communication structure. It provides an opportunity to more qualitatively unify the family and experience the individuality and uniqueness of each member. The psychotherapist, observing the "family sculpture," gains the ability to effectively influence the functioning of the family's specific features if necessary.

To create a complete "family sculpture," it sometimes only requires the participation of three or four people. Absent family members can be represented by other participants or by furniture chosen to symbolize their presence. At times, the therapist's position in the process can be metaphorically characterized as that of an identity "sculptor," and the therapy process itself is referred to as "sculpting," whereby the most balanced image is formed, capable of leading to constructive changes within the family system. Naturally, the changes introduced by the psychotherapist into the "family sculpture" are closely related to the verbal and non-verbal reactions of the family members.

Some therapists who employ Satir's method do not limit themselves solely to "sculpting" but also suggest that participants choose a phrase that could accurately characterize their present position and spatial location.

During the formation of the "family sculpture," the therapist may pose various questions aimed at increasing the family members' awareness of the observed situation. Some example questions include: "How do you feel in your current position in the 'family sculpture'?" "Are you surprised by what you are witnessing now?" "Did you know before that other family members perceive you in this way and not otherwise?" "When you look at the 'family sculpture,' do you perceive it as a reflection of the real situation in the family?" "How would you name the 'family sculpture' that we have created during the psychotherapeutic work?"

The "family sculpture" method can also be used in individual work. In this case, various objects can be symbolically used as substitutes for real people. However, it is worth noting that the group format of the work is preferable as it creates a more objective and accurate picture of the real situation, as well as a strong transformative process for all family members participating in therapy.

Virginia Satir formulated a set of beliefs that, in her opinion, reflect the therapist's position during the therapeutic process. She named these beliefs the "Five Freedoms." Let us consider them:

1. Freedom to see and hear what is here now instead of what could be or should be.
2. Freedom to express what I truly feel and think rather than what others expect.
3. Freedom to be oneself rather than wearing masks.
4. Freedom to ask for what is needed or necessary instead of waiting for permission.
5. Freedom to take responsibility for taking risks instead of acting in old stereotypical ways.

Satir believed that the key determining factor of our behavior is the family in which we grew up and the upbringing provided by our loved ones. She considered the family to be a system that seeks equilibrium in one way or another. The problematic aspects lie in the methods used to create this balance, while the underlying intentions are always pure. She acknowledged that any disruptions in the functioning of the family system give rise to low self-esteem and various forms of defensive behavior, which, in turn, pathologize the communicative context. Satir spoke about how every individual possesses sufficient internal resources to cope with the challenges life presents. She viewed the process of personal transformation as complex, systemic, and subject to specific rules and laws, understanding which enables therapy to be conducted at the highest level of effectiveness.

Upon examining Satir's beliefs, one can observe that many of them were borrowed by the creators of NLP for their practice and subsequently featured as "Presuppositions of NLP."

Bert Hellinger and Family Constellations

Bert Hellinger's family constellations represent a relatively new form of dramatic psychotherapeutic work. Hellinger, a German priest, philosopher, and psychotherapist, was born in Germany in 1925 into a Catholic family. At the age of ten, he studied at a Catholic boarding school affiliated with a monastery. In 1942, he was drafted into the army and fought on the Western Front. In 1945, he was taken as a prisoner of war and held in an Allied camp, but he later escaped and returned to Germany. He studied theology and philosophy at the University of Würzburg.

Bert Hellinger

After Hellinger took his priestly vows in 1952, he was sent to South Africa where he began missionary work among the Zulu tribes. While studying at the University of Pietermaritzburg and the University of South Africa, he earned a Bachelor of Arts degree and specialized as a schoolteacher, which he combined with his priestly activities for the next 16 years of his life in

South Africa. He served as the director of a school for the Zulu people and held administrative responsibility for a diocesan area consisting of 150 schools.

Hellinger spent a significant amount of time studying Zulu culture, their language, and participating in various rituals inherent to that culture. It is believed that many of the theoretical and practical insights he acquired from Zulu culture were later incorporated into his psychotherapeutic practice. In particular, it is known that some spiritual rituals of the Zulu people served as prototypes for his family constellations. This understanding suggests that the primary origins of the dramatic psychotherapeutic approach have a deeper and ancient source rather than being borrowed from Jacob Moreno's psychodrama, which is rooted not in shamanic ritual but in theatrical improvisation. However, upon closer examination, similarities can be observed in certain aspects between constellations and psychodrama. Nevertheless, they have very little in common in their theoretical and practical foundations, employing different principles of work and focusing on entirely different aspects.

At a certain stage of his work, Hellinger begins to change his philosophical beliefs and renounces his priesthood. Upon his return to Germany, he marries a woman named Gerda and then moves to Vienna, where he undergoes psychoanalytic training. After completing his training, he joins the Munich Association of Psychoanalysis. In 1973, Hellinger moves to California, USA, to study under the American psychotherapist Arthur Janov and his method of "Primal Scream," which he later practices in Germany. Hellinger recounts that initially he practiced the "Primal Scream" method in its original format, which lasted over nine months. Later, based on his observations, he shortened the course to three months and eventually to four weeks. Ultimately, he concluded that the technique itself could be conducted within a single psychotherapy session.

During a family constellations seminar held in Moscow, Hellinger demonstrated this form of work, which, to a large extent, could be classified as body therapy. He took a seated patient with both hands from both sides and gently pressed her against himself. Then he invited her to try moving forward as if she were crawling through a narrow tunnel. Several assistants began to help her do this, some pulling her from one side while others pushed from the other. After 5—10 minutes, she emerged from Hellinger's "embrace," which had triggered a significant age regression to the moment of birth in her consciousness. The assistants placed her next to the therapist on chairs, and she lay in his arms in a newborn baby state. Afterward, for more than 30 minutes, Hellinger verbally progressed her to her familiar age. In her consciousness, he created a visual metaphor of a staircase, where each step represented the next year of her life. At certain stages, she paused, and tears appeared. At one point, she even experienced vomiting. Hellinger commented on the emergence of various cathartic reactions in the patient's behavior as a reflection and expression of suppressed emotions during different periods of her development.

Hellinger later studied Eric Berne's Transactional Analysis, Neuro-Linguistic Programming (NLP) techniques, and Milton Erickson's hypnosis. From NLP techniques, we can see that Hellinger sometimes provides his patients with basic anchoring techniques. In his execution, the practice of Ericksonian hypnosis became more akin to a form of meditation. The meditations themselves integrate his understanding of the functioning principles of family systems and essentially represent a certain type of directive suggestion, performed in a very gentle form.

In the 1980s, he worked on creating a method of group psychotherapy based on drama. For a long time, this work remained backstage and was not widely discussed. Hellinger shares that he even considered retiring without fully developing his ideas into a comprehensive form of psychotherapeutic work. However, fate had other plans for his creation.

One of Bert Hellinger's students, German psychiatrist Gunthard Weber, in the early 1990s, proposed publishing a series of edited seminars where Hellinger presents the key positions of his method. The book was published in 1993 under the title "Love's Own Truth" and soon became a psychotherapeutic bestseller. Over the next 20 years, Hellinger wrote and published more than 70 books devoted to his therapeutic method. He also conducted training and psychotherapeutic seminars worldwide.

The process of family constellation unfolds in a format similar to Jacob Moreno's psychodrama and Virginia Satir's "family sculpture." A group of people gathers, and one person approaches the psychotherapist and states their request for work. The therapist briefly listens to the request and then selects different individuals from the group to serve as representatives for key figures or processes that need to be represented during the work.

Unlike other dramatic psychotherapeutic methods, the representative either receives minimal information about the role they will play or does not receive any information at all. Participants are then asked to pay attention to bodily sensations and the movements that arise within them. They are encouraged to move where they feel compelled and express the emotions that naturally want to be expressed.

Jacob Moreno's concept of "spontaneity" in this work is interpreted as the "movement of the soul" and relies more heavily on intuitive unconscious processes. The understanding of how role perception occurs draws on Rupert Sheldrake's theory of the morphic field—a unifying psychic space encompassing all living beings that contains necessary information. In Hellinger's perspective, the representative becomes a conduit for the information within this space.

The process of extracting information from the morphic field through the representative's work reflects a phenomenon that is scientifically underexplored. This aspect has subjected the method to numerous criticisms. However, despite this, a large number of psychotherapists have confirmed its effectiveness over many years. This method would not have gained such wide acceptance among the professional psychotherapy community if its key therapeutic aspects were knowingly based on false premises.

The movements of the representatives reflect specific and significant emotional processes existing within the emotional field to which the patient belongs. There can be numerous variations.

Let's describe some of them to highlight the general tendencies of the process.

- The downward movement of the representative reflects a general negative state, sometimes an illness, and sometimes the symbolic need to give a place to the deceased individuals with whom there is a connection.
- Sometimes, if the representative lies down, it indicates that the person whose role they are playing has already passed away or is in poor condition.
- If the representative in the constellations process attempts to leave the room where the group therapy is taking place,

it may reflect their unwillingness to live.

- If the representative rotates in place, it may indicate a sense of guilt.
- Continuously looking upward by the representative also signifies a sense of guilt.
- Looking downward by the representative indicates the need to include some deceased person related to the patient's dynamics in the constellation process. In such cases, the therapist selects another person from the group, asks them to lie down in the place where the other representative was looking, and starts experiencing the role.

The representative does not necessarily play the role of a specific person. Roles can reflect emotions, states, abstract processes, and phenomena. Roles can have names such as "Life," "Death," "Fate," "Power," "Illness," "Symptom," "Decision," "Resource," and so on. Different structural elements of the body, organs, and various processes occurring within them can also assume different roles. For example, during the constellation, the therapist may position the patient's representative, a diseased organ, and the illness.

According to Hellinger, the main roles that need to be actualized in the constellation at the beginning of the work should be closely related to the topic of the inquiry. The more secondary roles included in the constellation, the more convoluted and poorly interpretable the dynamics may become. Therefore, the principle of minimizing the inclusion of roles is employed. Only those elements that are extremely necessary for the manifestation of systemic dynamics are included.

The therapist usually asks the representatives to perform all movements slowly, without haste. They should express verbally what they feel in their bodies, without creating rationalizations. During the enactment of the role, representatives may experience intense emotions directly related to the emotional system of the patient they are working with. Once a participant exits the role, the emotional flow immediately ceases.

While embodying a role, the representative, who knows little or almost nothing about the patient's family, is capable of spontaneously actualizing not only various undifferentiated emotional experiences but also fragments of the patient's family system's past. Sometimes, very old fragments. For example, one of the authors of this text observed how a representative participating in a therapeutic session unexpectedly fell to the floor and started speaking about the sensation of vomiting masses coming out of him and choking on them. After some time, the surprised patient with whom the work was being done commented that this was exactly how his great-grandfather died. Such "reading" phenomena by the representative from the patient's emotional field occur quite often, and therapists sometimes accumulate dozens or hundreds of such stories. Again, despite their astonishing nature, these phenomena cannot yet be fully explained from a scientific paradigm perspective.

Bert Hellinger places significant emphasis on the system of relationships between the patient and their parents. He believes that any non-acceptance, resentment, or negative feelings that a person may transmit towards their parents can manifest as symptoms of varying complexity.

According to Hellinger, many problems in the family system arise due to a disruption of the existing hierarchy within the system. For example, when children look at their parents and begin to criticize their actions, such criticism eventually severs the connection between the child and the parent, depriving the child of the energy they could draw from that relationship.

Depending on the disruption of the connection with one or both parents, the quality of the symptoms can vary significantly. For instance, an emotional disconnection from the father often leads to problems with social integration. According to Hellinger, the figure of the father serves as a guide into the external world for an individual. A person who lacks an emotional connection with the maternal figure often experiences emotional problems associated with an inability to find peace and tranquility. Difficulties in the emotional connection with the mother are frequently the cause of drug and alcohol addiction.

Emotional connection with a parent is seen as the ability to accept what comes from them. However, unfortunately, it is not always easy to accept what comes from parents. Sometimes, it may seem impossible. At times, accepting both parents or one of them can become a lifelong challenge for an individual.

Organizational constellations are an intriguing variation of family constellations, where the focus of the therapist's attention shifts from the family system to the organizational system. This can involve a company, corporation, city, country, and so on. The functioning rules of organizational systems differ little from those of family systems, which is why all therapy methods for families can positively impact the effectiveness of a company's or any other organization's work.

During the process of creating an organizational constellation, substitutes are often selected to represent the company itself, the director, other employees, the problem, or challenge the company faces, and so on.

Let's provide an example of an organizational constellation we observed. The client consults the facilitator about specific financial difficulties experienced by the company, where the client is the director.

The facilitator selects representatives for the work, one of the key roles being that of "secrecy" related to the "symptom." The representative for "secrecy" lies down on the floor and reveals that they are dying in an unpleasant manner. The representative playing the role of money starts following the representative for "secrecy," lying down on the floor.

Subsequently, the facilitator asks the client if they know which deceased person, connected to the company, the financial flow may be following. The client responds that some time ago, before the financial decline, an unfortunate incident occurred in the company. Next to the company building, there was a small working space where an elderly security guard lived who died in a fire, likely due to excessive alcohol consumption. The company did not provide any support to the guard's family after his death. However, the "conscience" of the organizational system decided differently. The facilitator recommended to the director that they offer financial assistance to the family of the deceased, thereby embodying the positive intention behind the organization's symptom.

Sometimes, structural constellations are considered as a separate form of constellative work. In this form of work, the primary focus of attention is on various elements of the psyche, body, or any other system apart from the family and organizational systems.

For example, in a constellation, a representative of the patient and the organ that troubles them can be placed. Alternatively, a large number of organs can be gathered to observe how they manifest themselves through the behavior of representatives. These can be various elementary mental processes such as

31

intellect, memory, emotions, instincts, attention, perception, will, intention, and so on.

An interesting form of structural constellation can be used for planning and achieving different goals. For instance, representatives can play the roles of elements such as goals, resources, opportunities, information, obstacles, and others. In structural constellations, secrecy can be a crucial element, and its representative can intuitively begin to reveal what is hidden from the attention of both the client and the psychotherapist.

During organizational and structural constellation work, there is often a gradual shift of focus towards the family system of the client. It is because the family system serves as the carrier and prototype of what happens to an individual in other systems they belong to.

The relationships between larger and smaller social systems and their elements can be described through the concept of fractality, introduced in 1975 by the French and American mathematician Benoit Mandelbrot, the creator of fractal geometry. Mandelbrot defined a fractal as a set that possesses the property of self-similarity. That is, the whole has the same shape as one or more of its parts.

For example, the human body can be perceived as an element of the integrity of the family system and fractally reflect the processes occurring within it. This is why we can observe a correlation between relationship problems within families and physical illnesses. Similarly, we can trace the dependence of processes within larger social systems on processes occurring within family systems. For instance, if a large number of family systems belonging to a larger social system encounter similar problems, unresolved family issues will eventually become unresolved problems for the city, country, ethnic group, and so on.

In this case, we see that the family system serves as a kind of fractal link through which we can assess what can potentially happen at other fractal levels, whether larger or smaller, depending on the focus of attention.

At times, Bert Hellinger demonstrated in his work how the constellation process can be applied to very large social systems. For example, one representative plays the role of the ethnic group of Germans, while another represents Jews. In this case, the dynamics relate to more global social processes. Another interesting example is a constellation that Bert Hellinger demonstrated live while in Kyiv in 2010. During this work, he attempted to reconcile the psychic fields at a higher level between the Germans who attacked Ukraine during World War II and the Ukrainians and Russians who defended their country.

According to Hellinger, the processes occurring in large psychic fields constantly and intensely affect the functioning of family systems and the individuals within them.

Bert Hellinger's family constellations have borrowed many ideas from transgenerational psychotherapy, which postulates the inheritance of symptoms from one generation to another. For example, if a person experiences a certain disorder, therapy may focus on events from the personal experiences of the patient's parents, grandparents, or more distant relatives. Hellinger identifies the key relatives with whom a person has a very close psycho-emotional connection. These include the father, mother, grandparents, siblings, paternal and maternal siblings, and sometimes great-grandparents. It does not matter whether a person has had direct contact with them or has never seen them. According to Hellinger's beliefs, family remains family regardless of direct contact. The more significant and profound the events that may have occurred in the lives of certain family members, the greater the influence they can have on the well-being of individuals in subsequent generations.

For instance, Hellinger describes one of his cases in South America involving a young man suffering from schizophrenia. During the therapy process, it was revealed that his ancestors had been slave owners who had treated their slaves cruelly. In the constellation, a representative was chosen to represent the patient, as well as deceased slaves who had served his family. The representative for the patient lowered himself to lie next to the deceased slaves and remained there, expressing empathy for them. As a result, Hellinger believes that the patient's consciousness became fragmented.

Family members do not necessarily have to be blood relatives or sexual partners. They can also be individuals to whom someone from the family has shown great kindness or, conversely, inflicted significant harm.

Any strong influence one person has on another connects their family systems, and this connection can be enduring. It is sometimes referred to as "entanglement." The process of disentangling follows the rule of balance, which vividly demonstrates that everything we give to the world, we intuitively want to receive back. If we have given a lot, we desire to receive an equal amount in return. If we have caused harm, we want to compensate for it. If this does not occur consciously through actions aimed at compensation, a person may unconsciously seek to compensate for the harm through the manifestation of various symptoms on a psychological, physical, or social level. Feelings of guilt and shame, inherent to an individual, are interpreted by Hellinger as feelings of balance. He also believes that such feelings can lead to death through their manifestation

34

in symptoms.

It is crucial to note that feelings of guilt and shame are directly connected to the "conscience" that exists within the social systems to which an individual belongs. For instance, the collective conscience of Muslims allows them to have four wives without experiencing moral qualms about it. However, if Slavic men or women attempt to enter into similar types of social relationships, it is likely to lead to severe personal and emotional burnout. The conscience of a social system, internalized by each individual, sets the boundaries of what is acceptable and unacceptable in behavior and life as a whole. Because the consciences of different social systems can significantly differ, it can lead to conflicts between social systems, where a member of one system may harm members of another social system with a "clear conscience." We can observe numerous examples of such conflicts by exploring human history.

At the organizational level, we can see the manifestation of conscience, for example, in the "survivor syndrome," where only one person survives from a platoon of soldiers, who subsequently may experience profound anguish because they did not share the fate of their fallen comrades. This process of connection with the members of the system to which an individual belongs is called loyalty.

Similarly, family members can be loyal to each other in the manifestation of both positive events in a person's life and the manifestation of symptoms. In such cases, we can witness how, in the next generation, children begin to replicate various significant events from the lives of their ancestors. Loyalty in this case declares, "I am no better than others." Naturally, this process, in the vast majority of cases, has a deep unconscious nature and, when consciously recognized, can be subject to correction and transformation.

An interesting example of correcting this form of transgen-erational inheritance is described by NLP trainer Robert Dilts. His mother was diagnosed with stage IV breast cancer and was given a prognosis of approximately six months to live.

Dilts began verbal therapy with her, and some of the tech-niques he applied were directly related to the concepts of transgenerational psychotherapy. His maternal grandmother and great-grandmother also suffered from and died of cancer. He discovered that his mother held a deep unconscious belief that she was no better than her mother and grandmother, and therefore, she should follow them in illness and death.

Dilts reformed her beliefs in an elegant manner. He asked her to imagine herself first in the role of his grandmother, then as his great-grandmother, and then respond from their perspective about whether they wanted their child to suffer and die like them. She received a definitive answer: "No!" He anchored this state in his mother's consciousness, which apparently became one of the main reasons for her subsequent recovery.

After six months, her stage IV cancer went into complete remission. She lived for another 11 years after her recovery. It is worth noting that this reframing was one of the practices he applied to his mother. He also mentioned that part of her problem was a lack of purpose in life. Specifically, she had already achieved her goals. Her son and daughter were successful and self-actualized; her husband had passed away, and she didn't quite understand why she needed to continue living.

Dilts shared that he helped her form new goals to hold on to her life more firmly.

This story vividly illustrates how family conscience can create symptoms and how psychotherapeutic work can effectively correct such a process that contributes to the onset of illness.

Continuing the topic of schizophrenic disorder mentioned earlier, it is worth adding that Hellinger understands this condition as a manifestation of a specific conflict within the family system to which the patient belongs.

In fact, during his seminars, Hellinger even commented that he perceives schizophrenia not as an illness but as a process of one person in the family taking on the roles of both a killer and a victim. Through his work with patients suffering from schizophrenia using systemic constellations, he consistently observed a similar pattern. Their family systems had at least two roles that could not find reconciliation. Sometimes it could be the role of one killer and multiple victims. It is the simultaneous association with the roles of the killer and the victim that splits consciousness, according to Hellinger's opinion. The killer can come from either the same family or another family system. Ultimately, this does not significantly change the essence of the emotional processes in dynamics. The act of killing another person becomes a fact of their inclusion in the family system. Afterwards, someone will take on the role of the victim in the killer's family, just as someone will take on the role of the killer in the victim's family. This process is complementary.

The process of substitution is formed through empathy with the image introduced into the family system. If members of one system do not want to empathize with the attached role in the current generation, then in subsequent generations, someone will empathize with this image intensely. Sometimes, in constellation therapy for schizophrenia, the symptom can be shifted from a standstill, while other times the patient's association with the killer and victim images may be too strong. In such cases, we observe that, behind this symptom, like many others, lies love. The need within the family system to love what other members do not love. And, of course, this process is unconscious.

The first primary criterion that can somehow change the dynamics is the realization demonstrated in constellation work. The second criterion is the use of interventions that the therapist may recommend to the patient or other representatives. Often, the interventions themselves raise to the conscious level what is hidden in the unconscious through verbalization. In this way, the intervention weakens the symptom itself.processes that create movement in constellation work.

The third criterion may be targeted restructuring—reformulating the constellation process. It should be noted that in the early stages of the development of the family constellation method, Hellinger often performed restructuring. However, over time, he increasingly stopped exerting a rigid influence on the structure of the constellation, thus expressing trust in the systemic unconscious processes that create movement in constellation work.

Because of this, one can attempt to differentiate the technique of constellation work, as well as hypnosis, into directive and non-directive. Literally speaking, therapists practicing Hellinger's family constellations method do not make use of such a division. Nevertheless, in my opinion, such a classification seems to suggest itself.

The process of empathizing with what was previously devoid of empathy can manifest in various symptoms. Let's provide a few examples. The patient is a two-year-old child with sensory aphasia. During the consultation, the child's mother was present and described the situation in detail.

We gathered a detailed family history and discovered the following facts. The child's family—the maternal grandfather and grandmother—have been living in very difficult relation-ships for a long time but have not divorced. The grandfather has been unfaithful to the grandmother, and she has endured and not left him. Several years before the birth of our patient, the grandfather suffered a stroke, after which he developed severe speech problems. He lost his job and friends and leads a reclusive life, mainly spending time walking, reading, and watching television.

The grandmother does not empathize with him and may even take pleasure in his illness. Their daughter, the patient's mother, loves both her father and mother but has grown accustomed to empathizing with her mother and has shown little empathy toward her father.

In the dynamics of this system, we have discovered that the child sympathizes with the grandfather, whom almost no one sympathizes with. It is in this way that young children can interfere with family dynamics. Every member of the family needs sympathy. If, at the moment, no one sympathizes with a family member, then the next person who enters the family will most likely be the first to show them the necessary sympathy. In many ways, we can see here the embodiment of the rule that children will give space in their lives to what their parents do not want to acknowledge.A similar situation can arise when considering past sexual partners. Hellinger repeatedly emphasized that children often emotionally replace their parents' past sexual partners. For example, if a child's mother left a man before getting involved with the child's father and that man harbored strong resentment towards the woman, the child may start to resent the mother on his behalf. These are unconscious processes that govern the dynamics of family systems. From this, we can draw very interesting conclusions regarding the psychology and psychotherapy of relationships between men and women. It is important to consider the fact that any sexual partner we have had, to some extent, becomes connected to our family. Depending on how our relationship with them ends, our subsequent sexual relationships will take shape. If our previous partner resents us, the next partner will, to some extent, sooner or later resent us as well. The same applies in reverse. If the previous partner is grateful to us and experiences positive emotions, the next partner will sense it within the family field and react accordingly.

Naturally, a significant portion of the problems that arise within and outside the family system are directly related to a disruption in the balance of "giving and taking."

For example, in a partnership, if a man gives too much to his wife, it can destroy the relationship just as effectively as giving too little. The more one partner provides various goods of different qualities, the more the other partner will feel guilty about it.

The disruption of this balance can lead to various negative consequences. A man who gives too much to his wife will eventually betray her. It is worth noting that the perceptions of how much each partner should give and take from each other can significantly differ and be strongly influenced by the conscience of the ethnic and family systems to which the partners belong. This conscience embodies deep rules that the social system follows. If an individual, as part of this system, begins to violate these rules, it can produce various symptoms at the psychological, physical, and social levels.

Some symptoms in a person belonging to a family system can create a lack of empathy towards a particular family member. Stronger symptoms may arise in cases of hatred. Particularly intense symptoms occur when there is hatred towards deceased family members.

Let's consider an example from a supervision session conducted by Bert Hellinger at a seminar in Florida in 2003. A female psychotherapist approached him and shared a story about her patient who developed a very rare symptom after 35 years: elephantiasis. The symptom appeared after the patient decided to find her father, whom she had never seen before. She discovered his whereabouts and went to his house, but when she arrived, she found out that he had already passed away. After some time, the symptom began to actively manifest.

Hellinger conducted a constellation and placed two key elements in it: a representative for the patient and a representative for her deceased father. The patient's representative approached the father's representative and started yelling at him with fury. Her scream seemed somewhat insane. Hellinger immediately halted the constellation.

In this case, the symptom actively developed after the patient began to transmit the dormant hatred within her. The strong negative emotion became a trigger for her connection to her deceased father. In a way, she entered the "realm of the dead," while the symptom itself, which creates significant problems for spatial movement, prevented her from moving or rather, from moving into her father's home. In this case, the patient violated the rule of hierarchy by aggressively reacting to the father figure and disregarding the need to accept the deceased as they were.

Hatred towards the dead brings the hater closer to the dead, and the intensity of the feeling generates a certain symptom. In this situation, we observe another rule directly related to the dynamics of social systems: "We are free from what we accept as it is. What we hate enslaves us and holds us back." Hatred is a prison. Hatred towards a deceased family member is a prison with severe consequences.

A somewhat similar situation occurred in our private practice. A patient came to us who had never seen her father. During the course of psychotherapy, we discussed extensively the importance of establishing contact with the parental figure if it had not been established before. Hellinger believes that such contact can be highly beneficial for the child, regardless of the feedback received from the parental figure.

The patient found her father in another city, visited him, and established a connection. The contact was emotionally normal, and her father was glad to see her. However, the new wife of the father most likely was not. After seven months of communication, the father wrote to her that he could no longer stay in touch, terminating the contact. Presumably, this was at the request of his wife.

Our patient was overwhelmed with intense hatred. For several weeks after that, she experienced aggressive outbursts, and then, while riding a bicycle, she was involved in a hit-and-run accident. She was admitted to the hospital in serious condition with a fractured collarbone and a severe head injury. The head trauma was localized in the left temporal-parietal area of the brain, causing her to experience letter agnosia for the first four days after the injury. Ordinary text appeared to her as if it were written in a foreign language.

In this case, the intense hatred she felt towards her living father led to such an outcome.

Love and hatred are concepts that are somewhat similar in our psyche and physiology. Indifference, rather than love or hatred, represents their opposite.

Observing various patients, we repeatedly confirm the idea that hatred within a family gives rise to symptoms, and hatred towards deceased family members leads to very severe symptoms, both psychological and physical. Sometimes, symptoms manifest causally, at the level of cause and effect, when a person, after violating certain family rules to which they belong, feels drawn to situations where they may experience certain traumatic events.

Helinger reveals very interesting ideas regarding the emotional changes that need to occur within an individual before they are capable of establishing a fulfilling romantic connection with a person of the opposite sex. He explains that in order for a bond to be stable, a man needs to emotionally detach from his mother and move closer to his father figure. If this does not happen, the man's heart will be occupied by the mother figure, and he will be unable to form genuine relationships with women.

Based on our observations, men who are very close to their mother figure frequently engage in infidelity towards their partners. They are more inclined towards short-term relationships and often state that they cannot love or do not know what it means to love other women. These men also rarely desire marriage or children. In general, they exhibit irresponsibility in their sexual and partnership relationships. Excessive closeness to the mother figure often predisposes a man to criminal tendencies. All of our patients who, to some extent, were involved in criminal activities were "mommy's boys." The overwhelming majority of male patients who sought the services of prostitutes were also "mommy's boys."

However, we have also frequently observed that men who

are emotionally closer to their mothers can deeply immerse themselves in the religious, spiritual, and scientific spheres. In order to feel comfortable, the "mommy's boy" needs to rebel against existing rules and go beyond their boundaries. Naturally, going beyond these rules can have both constructive and destructive consequences. Therefore, the fate of a man belonging to this profile can be highly unpredictable. Yet the quality of their lives is directly linked to their ability to detach from the sphere of maternal influence.

The necessity of accepting parents as they are has nothing to do with blind compliance with their will. After reaching maturity, a person must learn to make decisions independently. We have observed numerous examples where adult men seeking advice from their mothers regarding complex life situations experienced a strong sense of helplessness. Overcoming this feeling can be achieved through distancing from the mother figure and symbolically or directly aligning oneself with the father figure. By being close to his father figure, a man gains social strength and the opportunity to effectively grow within society. Despite this rule, we have encountered a significant number of "mommy's boys" among our patients who have managed to achieve certain social heights. However, what unites them all is that their achievements were built upon the violation of moral or legal rules rather than their observance.

On the other hand, men who are emotionally closer to their father figure are more inclined to adhere to various social rules. They are often oriented toward family values and tend to be more orthodox. This applies to various spheres of life. "Mama's boys" and "daddy's boys" cannot understand each other. They often have completely different values and goals in life, with different vectors and focuses of attention. As an analogy, a "mama's boy" is more like the captain of a pirate ship, while a "daddy's boy" is the captain of a state ship. The "mama's boy" naturally gravitates towards women who are closer to the father figure, finding the connection he lacks.

A similar situation exists in the structure of relationships with parents for women, but with some modifications. If a man needs to distance himself from the mother and get closer to the father figure to mature, a woman needs to first distance herself from the mother and get closer to the father figure, learning how to maintain a psycho-emotional connection with him, and then move away from the father and get closer to the mother again.

If a woman remains emotionally attached to her father, there will be no room in her heart for another man. Such a woman will prefer short-term romances over long-term relationships. This preference can exist on both a conscious and unconscious level. In other words, a woman may consciously desire long-term relationships, but for some reason, they do not work out, and she intentionally changes sexual partners frequently.

The situation of a "daddy's daughter" becomes significantly exacerbated if the father is a socially significant person, holds a high position, or has other significant achievements. In our experience, in such cases, it is almost impossible for her to emotionally distance herself from her closeness to the father figure. Such a woman is capable of being in a long-term relationship only with a man who has lower status than her. However, if she persists in staying close to a high-status man while maintaining a strong emotional bond with her socially significant father, it will generate a strong conflict within her, which can manifest through symptoms of various qualities and directions.

Very often, such women find a husband who is significantly

less socially prominent than her and her father and start to cheat on their spouse. The less prominent husband is perceived as a complement to the father figure. If the father is cruel and aggressive, it often leads the "daddy's daughter" towards sexual promiscuity or even engaging in prostitution in various forms. The "daddy's daughter" always prefers "mama's boys" when searching for a partner, finding in them the connection they lack themselves. A long-lasting sexual bond between a "mama's boy" and a "daddy's daughter" is extremely rare. Only mutual emotional detachment from parents of the opposite sex can sustain and make it genuinely comfortable for both parties.

It is important to distinguish between the concepts of accepting a parent and being close to them. Accepting parents allows a child to establish a connection with the resources present in the family system, both masculine and feminine. Sometimes, due to various reasons, another family member may replace the lost parent. For example, a grandfather may act as a substitute for a father. In such cases, the child can effectively establish a connection with the image of masculine behavior. However, if the connection with the masculine or feminine image is completely lost within the family, the likelihood of neuroticization can significantly increase. In such circumstances, in order to rectify the situation, the child needs to find a new father or mother independently. By this, we mean a person who will serve as a role model for the child's desired type of behavior. There should be at least a minimally empathetic bond established between this person and the child. Then, the child will be able to integrate within themselves a complete image of masculine or feminine behavior.

Excessive closeness to a parent keeps a person's ego in a more infantile position, which will to some extent generate feelings of guilt. The older the person, the stronger the sense of guilt will be, which will shape other symptoms within their personality. For instance, male alcoholics and drug addicts often belong to the category of individuals who are excessively close to their mothers but do not fully accept them.

There is another interesting characteristic of our personality: we are capable of accepting a parent only when they maintain a certain distance from us. Being too close quickly turns into rejection. Increasing the distance allows acceptance to emerge but does not guarantee it. If we specify the appropriate and most suitable distance between a child and a parent, it is important to consider that it varies during different stages of development. The older the person, the greater the distance required for them to feel comfortable.Beliefs about the distance from the parental figure heavily depend on the conscience of the family and the ethnic system to which the person belongs. For example, in some families and cultures, a close bond between a child and their parents in adulthood may not evoke strong neurotic feelings, while in others, the dynamics can be diametrically opposite. Therefore, it is extremely challenging to establish clear criteria for the necessary distance. The emergence of certain symptoms serves as a calibration criterion for understanding the distance that needs to be established from the parent in order to improve the individual's condition.

Excessive closeness can generate the same symptoms as close distance. For example, the closer a man is to his mother, the more likely it is that he will prefer short-term relationships with women, probably avoiding marriage and fatherhood. His atti-tude towards women will be primarily sexual, lacking emotional closeness. Such men easily separate from women and often do not experience sentimental feelings about it. However, if the distance significantly increases, the man's attitude towards women can change dramatically. He will seek not a mistress but a wife, and marriage often becomes his primary goal in relationships with the opposite sex. These men genuinely desire children and express strong positive emotions upon their arrival. They do not shy away from responsibility. In general, this profile describes a husband rather than a lover.

However, different challenges arise in this case. Intense passion is rarely accessible to these men. Their love is more moderate, calm, and stable. Over time, the sexual attraction towards their permanent partner may diminish or even be completely reduced. On the contrary, it may increase towards other women, often leading to the search for a mistress. Nevertheless, the man continues to emotionally love his wife and rarely leaves her. This occurs due to the unconscious need of the man to transform his wife into the mother figure he lacks.

As a result of these processes, the dynamics of partnership relationships can be metaphorically represented as walking a tightrope, where a strong inclination in one direction or the other signifies a fall. Maintaining this balance to some extent is an art that can be learned by understanding the principles of family system dynamics.

Similar processes occur in women who are too close to their father figure. Such women are more consciously or unconsciously oriented towards sexual relationships than family and children. This profile corresponds more to that of a mistress than a wife.One vivid metaphor that effectively illustrates balanced parent-child relationships is the metaphor of our planetary system. Life on any planet is likely to emerge only if it is at a sufficient distance from the Sun for its warmth to foster life. If the distance is too great, it will be too cold, and the likelihood of life arising in such circumstances is also doubtful. In our view, this metaphor is highly applicable to describing relationships with parental figures who have the capacity to give life to their child while maintaining the appropriate distance.

Let us provide an interesting example from our work with patients. A 28-year-old man came to us with severe stuttering symptoms that had developed in early childhood. In our work with him, we discovered his strong attachment to the maternal figure, his dependence on her opinion, and a series of difficulties in asserting his own positions. Professionally, the patient is a doctor with excellent musical and programming skills. He has a developed and intellectual personality.

Through therapeutic work involving specific exercises from body-oriented therapy, we were able to quickly help him develop the ability to speak almost stutter-free. For instance, we provided him with breathing techniques and techniques of bodily response to emotions through hand strikes on a punching bag. The man was amazed by the changes that occurred in him. However, these changes were only short-lived. As soon as he returned home, where he lived with his mother, the symptoms returned.

He continued to come to us, and we regularly managed to demonstrate to him that body-oriented psychotherapy exercises could quickly and effectively restore his fluent speech. When the symptoms reappeared after some time, they did so with less intensity than before, but there was no complete recovery. We explained to him that the main part of the symptoms was being caused by excessive attachment to his mother and that full healing would only be possible if he significantly distanced himself from her. Several years later, our prognosis proved to be entirely accurate. He moved to Germany to work as an anesthesiologist, living there for some time. As a result of breaking the constant close bond with his mother, the symptoms diminished and eventually disappeared. When the patient returned to his hometown for a while and came to talk to us, his speech was fluent and rapid. There was nothing interrupting his thoughts. In this case, we can observe how effective it can be to maintain the necessary distance from a parent.

Another vivid metaphor that effectively illustrates balanced parent-child relationships is the metaphor of our planetary system. Life on any given planet is likely to emerge only if the planet is at a sufficient distance from the Sun, allowing its warmth to generate life. If the distance is too great, it will be cold, and the likelihood of life emerging in such a case is also doubtful. In my opinion, this metaphor is highly applicable to describe relationships with parental figures who can give life to their child while maintaining the proper and appropriate distance.

Let's provide a fascinating example from our work with patients. A 28-year-old man came to us with severe stuttering symptoms that had developed in early childhood. In our work with him, we discovered his strong attachment to the maternal figure, his dependence on her opinion, and a series of difficulties in asserting his own positions. Professionally, the patient is a doctor with excellent skills in music and programming. He has a developed and intellectual personality.

Through therapeutic work with specific exercises from body-oriented therapy, we were able to quickly develop his ability to speak almost without stuttering. For example, we provided him with breathing techniques and techniques of somatic emotional response through hand strikes on a punching bag. The man was amazed by the changes that occurred within him. However, the changes themselves were only short-lived. As soon as he returned home, where he lived with his mother, the symptoms resurfaced.

He continued coming to us, and we regularly demonstrated to him that body-oriented psychotherapy exercises could quickly and effectively restore his fluent speech. When the symptoms returned after a while, they were less intense than before, but complete healing did not occur. We explained to him that the main part of the symptoms was produced by hypercontact with his mother, and full recovery was only possible if he distanced himself significantly from her. Several years later, our prognosis was fully justified. He moved to Germany to work as an anesthesiologist and lived there for some time. Due to the disruption of his constant close bond with his mother, the symptoms diminished and eventually disappeared. When the patient returned to his hometown for a visit and came to talk to us, his speech was fluent and rapid. There was nothing in his consciousness that interrupted him. In this case, we can see how effective maintaining the necessary distance from the parent can be.

Therapeutic Intervention Model

This model is a set of speech patterns that a psychotherapist utters to the patient during the therapeutic process. Bert Hellinger defines these phrases as "strong," meaning they exert a significant influence on the conscious and unconscious processes of the patient when applied correctly by the psychotherapist.

The model comprises 12 different speech patterns, each serving various purposes. Sometimes the therapist utters the phrases while the patient simply listens, but a much more effective approach is for the patient to literally repeat the phrases. The patient does not necessarily need to fully comprehend the meaning of the phrases. They operate at a deep, abstract level, lifting and activating a significant part of the profound experience. Moreover, they possess a trance-like effect, making them interdisciplinary and applicable during hypnotic induction.

It is crucial to understand that it is the appropriateness of the phrase itself that can create the desired effect. Merely employing a straightforward, algorithmic approach guided by rational reasoning often fails to yield the expected substantial changes. These patterns can be easily utilized in independent therapeutic work. Meditations incorporating these patterns can have a profoundly transformative effect.

Delegation of Responsibility / Identity Perception

This pattern focuses on declaring a volitional impulse and delineating certain psychological and behavioral boundaries. It can activate unconscious processes that were previously stagnant or functioning improperly.

A crucial criterion is the delineation of emotional boundaries within the individual's personality. Often, if we fail to establish clear boundaries, our unconscious can behave unpredictably, frequently leading to discomfort and provoking uncontrollable behavior.

Examples of interventions based on this pattern include the following:

- **"I leave this here with you."** This intervention is applied in relation to individuals or the experiential space.
- **"I let go of this."** For instance, a problematic situation or experience.
- **"This is my/your/his/her/their responsibility."** This is applied to specific members of a family or organizational system to which the individual belongs.

In the latter case, various other terms can also be used, such as "experience," "emotions," "desires," "boundaries," "trauma," "pain," and others.

Boundaries can also be delineated in the following ways:

- **"You can sort this out among yourselves."** This intervention can be used, for example, when separating a child from negative feelings between conflicted parents. Quite often, on an unconscious level, the child interferes in the parents' conflict, even while formally remaining detached. Again, on an unconscious level, the child aligns with the side that provided more for them.

· **"I (identity), you (identity), they (identity)**." For example, "I am the son, you are the father, they are members of our family."

· **"Now you can speak for yourself**." Some explanation is required here. The formation of symptoms in an individual is often linked to a rejection of certain deceased or excluded family members. As a result, symptoms become a means of "speaking" for these rejected and excluded individuals to some extent. In the process of constellation work, after accepting such rejected individuals, this intervention may be appropriate. The acceptance itself can be facilitated through the phrase from the acceptance pattern: "**Now I see you**," and through the phrase from the inner space pattern: "**There is a place for you in my heart**."

· **"Living with the living, dead with the dead**." This phrase becomes relevant when, during the dynamics of constellation work, it is observed how images of deceased family members significantly interfere with the conscious and unconscious processes of the living.

· **"My place is with the living**." This phrase can be applied when an individual unconsciously attempts to align with deceased family members.

· **"I look at them for you**." For example, the dynamics may be as follows: if a parent does not want to look at a close family member, such as the father, the child will empathize with that person on a deep level, often manifesting it through various symptoms. In such cases, the child or a representative of the child in the constellation needs to say to the mother's representative, "**I look at him for you**." Verbalizing the deep unconscious process often changes it, making it more manageable and consequently less pathological.

- "**I make the decision – me/you/them**." This pattern helps declare and delineate zones of personal responsibility if they have been violated or incorrectly perceived.

Gratitude / Respect / Value

This pattern provides an opportunity to express feelings that, for various reasons, have not been realized. These interventions are excellent for summarizing various internal processes. These phrases can activate strong abreactive processes, releasing deeply blocked emotions.

Examples of interventions:

- "**Thank you for life**." This phrase is appropriate for parents or individuals who have saved the patient's life.
- "**I respect your boundaries**." This phrase can be applicable in various contexts, but we believe it can be particularly relevant when parents address their children.
- "**To me, you are the best (only one)**." This phrase can be used for many family members, often parents or more distant ancestors.
- "**You are my treasure**." It can be addressed to a group of individuals within the family or to the entire family system as a whole.
- "**I respect what you do**." Applicable to many family mem-

bers, often children addressing their parents.

The phrases we have listed, when applied in the appropriate context, can uplift the deep intention that may underlie a patient's symptom. Once verbalized, this intention loses some of its power or ceases to function altogether. Despite the apparent simplicity of these patterns, their impact can be astonishing.

Hierarchy / Equality

Within various social systems, there is always a distinct hierarchy determined by rules. Hellinger comments that those participants who entered the system earlier, who are older, and who adhere well to the system's rules, giving more than they take, potentially occupy a higher position in the hierarchy. There can be many examples of violating the systemic hierarchy, such as when a child places themselves above their parents, a younger sibling disrespects an older sibling, a subsequent sexual partner despises the previous one, and so on. In the case of violating the hierarchy of the system to which an individual belongs, they immediately feel a sense of guilt and shame. This process is directly influenced by the unconscious interaction of the individual with the members of the system. To exist comfortably within a particular family system, one needs to strive to understand the existing hierarchy. Observing the hierarchy deprives a person of feelings of guilt and thereby removes symptoms.

Examples of interventions can be found as follows:

· **"You are big, and I am small**." The intervention is directed from the child to the parents or more distant ancestors.

- **"You give, and I take**." The intervention is directed from the child to the parents or more distant ancestors, but often the focus is on the figures of the father and mother.
- **"You are equally good to me**." The intervention is most often directed by the child to both parents. This intervention can be particularly effective when the child excessively favors one parent. Typically, if a child does not empathize with one parent, they eventually take their place, replacing them. Sometimes the process of replacement can be halted through therapeutic work, including the use of phrases from this model. However, in some cases, the process of replacement has a deeper nature, and therapeutic work can do little to change it. Rather, it can set the direction for therapy that the patient may pick up.
- **"Now you are one of us**." This phrase is used when a particular family member has been excluded and then returned.
- **"With you, we are equals**." The phrase is appropriate in relation to any family member who occupies an equal hierarchical position. For example, from a husband to a wife.

Planning the Future

The application of this pattern provides an opportunity to create a more conscious perception of future events and direct a person's behavior and emotions in the desired direction. Emotional connection with the future also provides additional support for the individual, allowing for more rational thinking and action.

Examples of interventions can be found as follows:

- **"Now I will do something good with this**." This intervention is relevant when therapy reveals a negative situation that, in a literal sense, cannot be resolved.
- **"I will remember**." This is applicable in relation to any negative past experiences within the family system.
- **"I will accept everything you reveal**." This phrase expresses readiness to accept the secrets of a family member and shows respect for them.
- **"I will take care of myself**." The phrase is directed from children to parents or more distant family members, and it can be a promise.

Acceptance of the Present

Different phrases about accepting and acknowledging the present can allow for a more vivid and accurate awareness of the situation. These phrases can also serve as truisms – truths that are difficult to consciously resist, making them even more trance-inducing.

Examples of interventions:

- **"I have come to terms with this**." The phrase implies accepting the situation in the family system as it is. Only after that is it possible to take any action.
- **"I accept you as you are**." Similar to the previous phrase, but the focus of attention is on a specific individual within the family system.
- **"Now you are with us**." The phrase is about accepting family members who were previously excluded.

- **"This is part of life."** The phrase is about accepting the situation as it is with the maximum generalization to the entire life context.

As Bert Hellinger said, "What we reject holds us back. What we accept sets us free." These phrases bring us as close as possible to the practical embodiment of this belief.

Acceptance of the Past

Acknowledging and accepting the past is just as important as accepting the future and the present. Until a person is able to accept their past, it holds them back and prevents them from moving forward. However, acceptance in this case means agreement and readiness to properly conclude what was left unfinished.

Examples of interventions:

- **"I ran away from you."** This phrase is directed toward significant family members from older generations. It is spoken when a descendant, for various reasons, avoids their ancestors.
- **"I shared the responsibility/emotion/secret."** This phrase acknowledges the process of specific bonding between family members in the past.
- **"You were forgotten."** This phrase is directed at a specific family member who was excluded in the past for various reasons.

Acknowledgment of Perception / Thinking / Emotion

This pattern allows for a deeper awareness of various psychological processes that may be actualized during the therapeutic process. Consciously actualizing these psychological processes allows for a better understanding, management, and control of them. Additionally, uttering these interventions can create a connection between fragmented experiences that were previously unconnected for various reasons.

Examples of interventions:

- **"Now I see you."** This can be applicable to any family member, living or deceased, who, for some reason, was not the focus of attention.
- **"I don't know your depths."** This phrase acknowledges the fact that some of the patient's ancestors may have had secrets that cannot currently be revealed for various reasons. It also creates an atmosphere of acceptance and respect for the person it is directed at.
- **"This is the truth."** The phrase is aimed at acknowledging certain facts related to the family system that were hidden or ignored for various reasons.
- **"For me, this is happiness."** Any integrative processes occurring within the family system, consciously or unconsciously, can be significantly enhanced by this phrase.

Internal Space Allocation

A person's symptoms are directly related to their resistance to various processes in life, circumstances, people, emotions, and so on. The longer we fail to accept someone or something from our family system, the more the fact of non-acceptance creates a certain alternative that we cannot ignore. Sometimes, acceptance itself requires time and a certain transformation of personality, without which proper integration may be impossible.

These phrases create an important vector of conscious movement that, under certain appropriate circumstances, can yield magnificent results. One of the particularly strong observed consequences of these phrases is a sense of relief and tranquility. Sometimes a person's anger and resentment towards others prevent them from reconciling with themselves by accepting certain facts of reality. In such cases, it is necessary to release the situation and allow the patient to make the decision on their own.

Examples of interventions:

- "**For you/you all/this, there is a place in my heart**." This phrase can be directed towards any family member, a group of people within the family, significant emotional processes, or current events.
- "**For you, there is a special place in my heart**." This phrase serves the same function as the previous one but, among other things, emphasizes the particular significance of a specific element within the system. This can be important, for example, in relation to a person in the family who has been excluded and unaccepted for a long time. The balance rule in the family system states that the more something is rejected, the more persistently it will be accepted. Quite often, we can observe a pattern of non-acceptance and acceptance spanning several generations. For instance, what parents strongly reject, their children start actualizing.

61

In this process, the family system finds balance. However, it should be noted that balance cannot be achieved without understanding polarities.

- **"You also have a right to a voice within me."** This phrase is aimed at the conscious actualization of the process of manifesting someone who has been excluded from the family system through the patient's consciousness and body. Uttering this phrase can partially or completely weaken the symptom's power.

- **"Only you are dear to me. There is no place in my heart for others."** Sometimes, certain images of deceased family members become the primary focus of the patient's unconscious processes. Sometimes the person may be aware of this, sometimes not. The best way to rectify the situation is to give the image what it wants. That is, verbally accentuate its maximum value. Afterwards, the dynamics usually change, partially or completely. However, if significant changes do not occur, it is pointless to force the situation. The intervention sets the vector of consciousness movement, and further actions should be left to the wisdom of the family unconscious.

- **"You will always live in my heart."** This phrase allows for emphasizing that the act of acceptance will also take place in the future. Such an action usually leads to a deeper integration of meanings.

Request

Requests and blessings have the ability to actualize and align hierarchical positions within the family system, initiate the correct vector of emotional processes, and unleash the potential of current resources. The provided phrases are particularly effective when directed at family members from older generations.

Examples of interventions:

- **"Please."** This phrase can be relevant when addressing an older relative who may be upset with the patient for something or simply not paying attention to them.
- **"I request you."** The purpose of this phrase is similar to the previous one.

Blessing

Phrases requesting blessings have the power to establish or enhance the connection between younger and older generations. Hellinger commented on his understanding of good parents and good children. In his view, a good parent is one who is capable of giving, while a good child is one who is capable of receiving.

Parents pass on specific resources to their children, which can be perceived by the children as either something good or something bad. However, if a child is able to perceive what comes from their parents as a blessing, it empowers them. Rejecting what comes from the parents weakens a person. But it's important to remember that literal acceptance is not mandatory. The child can transform everything they have received in their own way. In ancient alchemy, this process was called "sublimation" — the alchemists referred to it as the process of turning lead into gold, that is, transforming something base into something noble.

Unfortunately, not all children receive "gold" from their parents. But if a child can independently turn "lead" into "gold," it significantly strengthens them. Merely rejecting the "lead" yields no fruit. The best choice is to accept what comes and, if it is disliked, subject it to transformation, processing, and subsequent assimilation.

Examples of interventions:

- **"Bless me."** This phrase is uttered by a child in relation to their parents or older relatives.
- **"I bless you."** This phrase is spoken by a member of the older generation towards someone from the younger generation.
- **"Peace be with you."** This phrase can be directed at various family members or their group. It is worth noting that this phrase has the ability to create a sense of proper completion of a particular process within the family system.

Accentuation of Value

Assigning significance to important systemic processes occurring within the family system strengthens them and makes them more resilient. When the significance of certain important aspects or parts of the family system is not emphasized, some or all family members will take responsibility for it, and this will manifest in various symptoms. Each element of the family system plays an important role. Some elements may be more coherent and balanced, while others may exhibit different symptoms. However, the coherence of some elements and the symptoms of other family members are interconnected and dependent on each other. Therefore, each element of the family system holds value. Naturally, these values can have different meanings.

Examples of interventions:

- **"Dear (father, mother, son, daughter, etc.)"** This phrase directly accentuates the significance of a specific family member.
- **"I value you."** This phrase conveys a similar meaning to the previous one and serves as its logical continuation.
- **"You are priceless."** This phrase places special emphasis on significance. It is appropriate when referring to a person who has been excluded from the family system for an extended period.

Indication of Perception / Action

Phrases of this pattern emphasize the transformative process that may occur in the patient during therapeutic work. They reinforce it, contribute to the patient's growing confidence in the correctness of what is happening, and actualize a more intense expression of suppressed emotions.

Examples of interventions:

- **"Just observe/listen/feel/absorb/breathe."** This phrase is suitable for any transformative process within the context of therapy.
- **"Allow your body to surprise you."** This phrase is effective when a moment of revelation occurs in therapy, revealing a mystery that has not been expressed for various reasons.
- **"Just let this have an impact."** This phrase is useful when the patient has already gained some experience in the therapeutic process but has not fully grasped it yet.
- **"Open your heart to everything that lies between you, and begin to grow together."** This phrase initiates deep processes of assimilation and integration of the experiences

observed by the patient within the therapeutic context.

Pathopsychological Profiles and Drama Therapy

It is worth noting from the outset that drama therapy in psychotherapy is one of the most suitable approaches for almost all pathopsychological profiles. The variations lie more in the details of how each profile representative reacts to the process of dramatic therapy.

Hysteroid Profile

For hysteroid patients, participation in the dramatic form of psychotherapy is often perceived as being in their element. Hysteroids themselves are actors, and here they are provided with such a splendid sublimation context. However, practicing therapists should not forget that some of the emotional and behavioral reactions to histrionics involve exaggeration and sometimes even falsehood. Based on our experience, histrionic personalities almost always create the greatest impact on the audience in the dramatic form of psychotherapy. Some cases of working with such patients can leave a deep impression and be remembered for years. Moreover, in my opinion, the dramatic approach to working with histrionic patients becomes effective only when the therapist can identify the patient's true emotional reactions, a skill that comes with time and consistent practice. It is important to always remember that, on a deeper level, histrionics are not interested in concluding therapy, especially in a dramatic manner. Just as an actor is unlikely to want to end their career after a good performance, a histrionic is interested in creating a strong emotional impact on others. However, most of their games operate on an unconscious level.

Paranoid Profile

For paranoid patients, immersion in dramatic forms of therapy is rare. The presence of unfamiliar or little-known individuals often triggers anxiety and distress in them. The ability for open and sincere communication also significantly suffers. Paranoid individuals may constantly believe that anything others see or hear about them during group work will eventually be used against them. It is virtually impossible to convince such personalities otherwise. However, if paranoid reactions are not exaggerated, a paranoid individual can gain valuable and significant insight through dramatic therapy.

Psychopathic Profile

In our observation, pure psychopaths will ignore the opportunity to participate in dramatic group work. If they do participate, they often have a poor understanding of what is happening before them due to problems with abstract thinking. A psychopath usually cannot grasp the abstract core of a dramatic session, making it difficult for them to draw any conclusions for themselves from what they have seen, heard, and felt. Much more often, in a dramatic group, one can find patients with a mixed pathopsychological profile, where psychopathy comes along with, for example, a histrionic profile. The combination of psychopathic and histrionic profiles can occasionally be seen in dramatic groups, while other combinations are extremely rare.

Obsessive-Compulsive Profile

According to our observations, individuals with an obsessive-compulsive personality adapt excellently to the dramatic therapeutic process and draw numerous insights and inspiration from it. Participation in a dramatic session can deeply address their problems at times. Patients with this profile usually do not exhibit strong resistance to this form of psychotherapy.

Schizoid Profile

Initially, individuals with schizoid personality often experience difficulties adapting to the dramatic context. However, as they realize that they are accepted in the group, they begin to behave differently. This is closely related to the intensity of schizoid manifestations. The more intense they are, the slower the adaptation process becomes. We have observed various examples of behavior and dynamics among schizoids in dramatic groups. Some may consistently attend sessions for a year or more, while others may only participate once or a few times. We have discovered that the dramatic group can have positive effects on schizoid personalities, particularly if they remain in the group for a longer period. However, even a single session can provide an opportunity for better self-understanding.

Epileptoid Profile

According to our observations, individuals with an epileptoid personality feel great after dramatic therapy. They are not prone to excessive dramatization like histrionics, excel in playing assigned roles, and are highly receptive to the information received during therapy. We have found that dramatic therapy is one of the best forms of therapeutic work for epileptoid personalities. However, it depends on the individual and other personality characteristics.

Manic-Depressive Profile

Bipolar patients are highly responsive to dramatic works and can easily assimilate psychotherapeutic material. However, in my opinion, dramas are sometimes insufficient for them to reach the core emotions underlying their personality profile. More rigid, abreactive cathartic methods are likely required, which can be applied in parallel with dramatic works. However, manic-depressive patients most often appear in a dramatic session during the manic phase when they accumulate a lot of energy. Sometimes they may join the group during the interphase. During the depressive phase, patients are usually unable to motivate themselves to attend therapy in general, and specifically the dramatic form of it.

A Brief Message from the Author

Mastering complex psychotherapeutic theories and practices can be a challenging journey. By sharing your experience with this book, you can guide others who are on the same path. Your review could inspire someone to take the next step in deepening their knowledge and applying these insights to make meaningful changes in their life.

Thank you for your support and for taking the time to share your thoughts! Your feedback helps us refine our offerings and empowers others in their pursuit of mastering psychotherapy. If this book has been valuable to you, I'd be grateful if you could take a moment to leave a review. **Your positive rating would mean a lot!**

To share your feedback, simply scan the QR code or click the link below:

psychemaster.com/recommends/review-drama-therapy

Bibliography

1. Moreno, J. L. (2001). Psychodrama. Moscow: "April Press"; "Eksmo-Press." (Translated by G. Pimochkina, E. Rachkova)

2. Moreno, J. L. (2001). Sociometry: Experimental method and the science of society. Moscow: "Academic Project." (Translated by A. Bokovikov, Ed. by R. A. Zolotovitsky)

3. Moreno, J. (1993). Theatre of Spontaneity. Krasnoyarsk: Mental Health Foundation. (Translated by B. I. Khasan)

4. Satir, V. (2007). You and Your Family. Moscow: April-Press, Institute of General Humanities Studies.

5. Satir, V. (1992). How to Build Yourself and Your Family. Moscow: Pedagogika-Press.

6. Satir, V. (2001). Family Therapy. Moscow: Speech.

7. Satir, V. (2009). Family Therapy: A Practical Guide. Moscow: Institute of General Humanities Studies.

8. Satir, V., Bandler, R., Grindler, D. (2000). Family Therapy and NLP. Moscow: Institute of General Humanities Studies.

9. Hellinger, B. (2006). And It Becomes Easy in the Middle of You. Book for Those Who Want to Find Harmony in Relationships, Love, and Happiness. (2nd ed.). Moscow: Institute of Counseling and Systemic Solutions, Institute of Psychotherapy Publishing House.

10. Hellinger, B. (2015). Success Stories in Life and Profession.

Kyiv: Hellinger Publications.

11. Hellinger, B. (2005). The Source Doesn't Need to Ask for Paths. Moscow: Institute of Counseling and Systemic Solutions, Higher School of Psychology.

12. Hellinger, B. (2009). Love of the Spirit. Moscow: Institute of Counseling and Systemic Solutions.

13. Hellinger, B. (2007). We Are Moving Forward. Course for Couples in Difficult Situations. Moscow: Institute of Counseling and Systemic Solutions.

14. Hellinger, B. (2007). Orders of Love: Resolving Systemic and Family Conflicts and Contradictions. Moscow: Institute of Psychotherapy Publishing House. (Translated by Diana Komlach)

15. Hellinger, B. (2006). Orders of Help. Moscow: Institute of Counseling and Systemic Solutions.

16. Hellinger, B. (2009). Happiness That Remains. Moscow: Institute of Counseling and Systemic Solutions.

17. Hellinger, B. (2010). Success in Life / Success in Profession. Kyiv: Hellinger Publications.

About the Author

Dr. **Artem Kudelia**, a psychologist with a PhD and a practicing therapist, has extensive expertise in integrative approaches. He possesses comprehensive knowledge of a wide range of psychotherapeutic methods, including humanistic and existential theories, as well as the practical application of cognitive-behavioral therapy (CBT) to effectively address issues such as anxiety, depression, obsessive thoughts, compulsions, social phobias, and complex emotions. His books are valuable resources for professionals and individuals interested in managing their mental health. In addition to managing symptoms, he helps his clients toward self-actualization in various aspects of their lives, including social, career, and personal aspects.

You can connect with me on:
- 🔗 https://facebook.com/psyche.masters
- 🔗 https://instagram.com/psyche.masters
- 🔗 https://threads.net/@psyche.masters
- 🔗 https://youtube.com/@psyche.masters
- 🔗 https://tiktok.com/@psyche.masters
- 🔗 https://pinterest.com/psychemasters

Subscribe to my newsletter:
- ✉ https://psychemaster.com/early-reader-signup

Also by Artem Kudelia PhD

The *Psychology & Psychotherapy Theories & Practices* series offers a detailed examination of the history, theoretical foundations, and practical applications of fundamental approaches in psychotherapy. It is an indispensable resource for psychologists, medical professionals, psychology students, and anyone interested in understanding these complex subjects.

Additionally, the *Cognitive Behavioral Therapy Self-Help Guide: 15 Steps to Mental Health* series provides actionable guidance for overcoming various psychological challenges, such as anxiety, depression, excessive anger, obsessive thoughts, compulsions, social phobias, health anxiety, and intricate emotional struggles. These topics were chosen because many individuals facing these challenges often lack awareness of the underlying dynamics. By gaining insight into these processes, individuals can make informed decisions about seeking help, reinforcing the idea that knowledge is a powerful tool for personal empowerment.

Together, these series offer invaluable resources for those interested in psychology, whether for academic study or personal development, by providing comprehensive insights and practical tools that contribute to improved mental well-being.

**Psychotherapy Fundamentals
Complete Guide**

Are you struggling to understand complex psychotherapeutic theories?

Discover a streamlined approach to mastering psychotherapy concepts and practical applications in just 4 weeks.

Psychotherapy Fundamentals: Complete Guide simplifies the intricate world of psychotherapy, making it accessible and actionable for those interested in self-discovery, self-education, and readers with a wide range of interests.

♥ **Imagine confidently navigating psychotherapeutic real-world scenarios with ease.**

This book is your **comprehensive roadmap to achieving a deep and practical understanding of psychotherapy**. You'll learn to simplify complex theories and integrate them effectively into your life and practice.

Gain a comprehensive understanding of various therapeutic approaches, including **provocative** therapy, **humanistic** therapy, **somatic** therapy, **existential** therapy, **drama** therapy, **psychedelic** and **post-psychedelic** therapy, **anti-psychiatric** therapy, and **integrative** therapy. Each chapter delves into the key themes and methods of these psychotherapy modalities, broadening the horizons for those interested in self-discovery, self-education, and lifelong learning.

Hypnotherapy Fundamentals
Complete Guide

Are you ready to uncover the secrets of hypnotherapy?

This comprehensive guide immerses you in the theory and history of hypnosis, providing a solid foundation for understanding the principles underlying hypnotherapy.

Explore the various techniques and approaches used in hypnotherapy training, including the art of suggestion and deepening hypnotic trance states, the creation of therapeutic propositions, and the utilization of the power of the subconscious mind.

Learn how to effectively apply hypnotherapy techniques to address a wide range of issues, from managing stress and anxiety to overcoming phobias and habits.

Gain an understanding of the transformative potential of hypnosis and its applications for personal growth and well-being.

Unlock the secrets of harnessing the power of the mind and creating positive changes in yourself and others.

Psychology of Love & Death
Therapeutic Path to Fundamental Balance
in Life and Relationships

How to Achieve Fundamental Balance in Life and Relationships?

Explore dualistic nature of human consciousness, along with the profound impact of seeking balance between fundamental continuums of **love and death**, **instinct and spirituality**, **masculinity and femininity** in shaping our experiences and relationships.

Explore the psychopathological profiles and manifestations of love and death, including profiles such as hysteria, paranoia, psychopathy, and others.

Uncover different types of love, from **eros** to **agape**, and study the **three-component Theory of Love**.

Familiarize yourself with **real-life psychotherapy cases** that illustrate the complexities of love, death, and therapy and gain **valuable insights** into the human experience and its challenges.

Cognitive Behavioral Therapy
Managing Anxiety and Depression

Explore the roots of anxiety and learn why it's a fundamental aspect of the human experience.

An in-depth exploration of **Panic Disorder**, addressing the irrational fears associated with it.

Examine the nuances of **Social Anxiety** and its impact on personal and professional spheres.

Dive into the world of **Obsessive-Compulsive Disorder**, unraveling its complexities.

Understand the genetic predispositions and learn effective strategies to manage obsessions and compulsions.

Explore **PTSD** from its roots to its biological manifestations. Delve into the trauma cycles, and discover therapeutic techniques for stabilization and overcoming trauma.

Grasp the degrees of **Depression**, from mild to severe, debunking common myths.

Breathwork Therapy Seminar
Holotropic Journey to Unconscious Mind
Secrets

Tap Into the Wisdom of Transpersonal Psychology!

This book is the <u>transcript of a seminar</u> that addresses the profound questions of **subconsciousness**, offering a unique perspective on personal growth and healing.

Gain profound insights into the workings of your mind and explore the mysteries of human consciousness.

Access practical exercises and techniques to facilitate personal growth, healing, and self-awareness.

Written for seekers of self-awareness, psychology enthusiasts, and anyone curious about the depths of the human mind.

Explore the integration of spirituality and psychology, uncovering your inner potential.

Psychotherapy
Introduction to Healing Vectors

Do you want to understand the variety of methods of psychotherapy and choose the one that is best for you?

In the vast world of psycho-technologies, there are numerous methods of psychotherapy that encompass a wide range of personality theories and concepts.

Drawing upon an integral framework, the book maps out the complex landscape of psychotherapy, encompassing vectors such as psychoanalytic, hypnotic, provocative, humanistic, behavioral, existential, transpersonal, cognitive, somatic, psychodramatic and psychedelic therapies, among many others.

This book will provide you with valuable knowledge that will allow you to choose the most suitable therapeutic path for specific circumstances and personality types.

Provocative Therapy
The Healing Power of Dark Humor

Who said that psychotherapy can't be hilariously funny?

Explore innovative ideas about the power of humor in psychotherapy and coaching.

Uncover the archetypal foundation of Provocative Therapy inspired by the myths of the Trickster and the Holy Fool.

Delve into the transformational potential of **Group Provocative Psychotherapy** and the important rules that define successful group dynamics.

Explore the effectiveness of **Provocative Coaching** and its focus points.

Dive into the fascinating world of **Provocative Drama** and its role in therapeutic interventions.

Explore the **pathopsychological profiles**, including **hysteroid**, **paranoid**, **psychopathic**, **obsessive-compulsive**, **schizoid**, **epileptoid**, **schizophrenic**, and **manic-depressive** profiles.

Humanistic Therapy
From Crisis to Self-Actualization

Do you want to explore a world where people are seen as unique holistic systems with infinite potential waiting to be discovered?

Immerse yourself in the theories and practices of humanistic therapy and explore the **transformative path from crisis to self-actualization**.

Unlike psychoanalysis, which focuses on internal complexes and personal traumas, humanistic therapy emphasizes the **study and development of positive personality qualities**.

Humanistic philosophy has also influenced fields such as **education**, promoting **empathy** and **support** as the foundation of learning.

This holistic approach recognizes the **interconnectedness of mind, body, and spirit** and seeks to stimulate personal **growth** and **well-being**.

Take the first step towards self-awareness, personal growth, and a more fulfilling existence.

Somatic Therapy
The Wisdom of the Body

Would you like to establish a connection with your body and access the source of wisdom?

Unleash the transformative power of **somatic therapy** and embark on a journey of **self-discovery** and **healing**.

Explore the profound connection between the **mind and body**.

Discover the **seven levels of muscular armor** and their connection to specific emotions such as sadness, anger, and fear.

By exploring different body segments, you will unlock **powerful techniques** for releasing pent-up emotions and promoting harmony throughout the organism. From **eye movements** and **jaw exercises** to **deep breathing** and **body movements**, this book offers **practical methods** for **accessing the wisdom of the body** and **restoring emotional balance**.

Acquire unique knowledge about **healing after birth trauma and psychosomatic medicine**.

**Existential Therapy
Journey to Authenticity**

*Do you want to know who you really are?
What is your personal meaning of existence?*

Embark on a **transformative journey** to uncover your **true essence** and embrace the **principles** of existential therapy.

Explore the rich philosophical roots of **existential psychotherapy** and find your path to **personal authenticity**.

Explore key themes such as **freedom, responsibility, meaning**, and **choice**, and learn to courageously and authentically navigate the complexities of existence.

This book provides **practical ideas and techniques** for **applying the principles of existential therapy** to your own life.

Gain a deep **understanding** of your **values, beliefs**, and **desires**, and learn to **embrace uncertainty** and **transform** life's **challenges** into **opportunities** for **growth** and **self-discovery**.

Psychedelic Therapy
The Healing Power Therapeutic Journeys

Embark on a transformative journey into the world of psychedelic therapy!

Explore the fascinating **history** of **psychedelic substances** and potential benefits of working with consciousness-altering substances in clinical practice.

Learn comprehensive information on various **psychedelic therapies**, including **ketamine therapy**, **psilocybin**-assisted psychotherapy, **MDMA**-assisted psychotherapy, and **ibogaine** psychotherapy.

Gain knowledge about **mental health** in the **perinatal period**, the **role of hypnosis**, and the transformative power of **holotropic breathwork**.

Understand the profound impact of **psychedelic medicine** and the potential of **psilocybin microdosing**.

Explore the therapeutic applications of **ketamine** in the **treatment of depression** and **psychosynthesis in coaching**.

Beyond Psychiatry
Exploring Anti-Psychiatry Method

Challenge traditional psychiatry and psy-chotherapy!

This book presents an **alternative to conventional** ideas of normalcy and offers a **fresh perspective on psychological disorders**, inviting readers to question existing paradigms.

Delve deeper into **psychopathological profiles** and **anti-psychiatric** forms of psychotherapy, examining various profiles including **hysteria, paranoia, psychopathy,** and more.

Gain an understanding of the intersection of psychotherapy and existential philosophy, **challenging the myth of mental illness** within families.

Explore the **treatment of psychosis, trauma,** and **emotional disorders from a holistic perspective**.

**Integrative Therapy
Personal Transformation Guide**

Discover the Power of Integrative Therapy and Embark on a Journey of Personal Transformation!

This book challenges traditional divisions in **therapeutic approaches** and explores the potential of **combining multiple vectors** to create a **comprehensive and integrated therapeutic system**.

Immerse yourself in the world of neuro-linguistic programming (NLP), **cognitive styles**, **neurological levels**, and **integral philosophy**, among other concepts.

Explore practical methodologies such as shifting negative thinking, **creating rapport**, and using linguistic patterns to facilitate positive change.

Unlock the transformative **power of anchors**, **changing personal history** and submodalities.

Gain an understanding of maps of the world and the **metamodel** for **effective communication**.

Theory & History of Hypnosis
Exploring Altered State of Mind in Trance

Immerse yourself in the fascinating world of hypnosis and explore the <u>history and theory</u> of altered states of consciousness!

This book sheds light on **historical trance practices** and the **role of shamanism**, tracing its influence on **modern psychospiritual orientations**.

Discover the benefits of this book by exploring the **history of trance practices and hypnotherapy**.

Explore the **evolution** of **shamanism**, its connection to **religion**, and its pre-religious **philosophy**, which offered deep insights into the structure of the universe and the mysteries of the spiritual world.

Discover various **hypnotic phenomena** and **states of consciousness** that can be induced in a trance state.

Explore their potential applications in **psychotherapeutic practice**, from **pain management** to the **treatment of depression**.

Learn techniques such as **self-hypnosis**, **deep trance induction**, and **guided healing visualizations**.

Hypnotherapy Training
A Guide for Practicing Hypnotherapists

Uncover the secrets of hypnotherapy and improve your <u>practical hypnosis skills</u>!

This book explores techniques and practical skills for hypnotherapists.

Dive into the depths of the subconscious and discover the transformative potential of hypnotherapy.

Discover the benefits of this book, which delves into key topics and approaches in hypnotherapy training.

Explore developed techniques, including rapport-building practices and the use of matching postures, movements, and breathing with the client.

Unveil the levels of depth in hypnotic trance and the model of trance levels.

Engage in exercises that enable the attainment of different trance levels and explore the motives of trance and their application in psychotherapy.

Gain an understanding of different styles and orientations of hypnotic work, from hypnoanalytic and suggestive to behavioral and transpersonal.

**Healing Anxiety and Overthinking
Proven CBT Strategies for Lasting Relief**

Are you exhausted from the relentless cycle of anxiety and overthinking?

Discover the 15-step program that will transform your mental health and bring peace of mind.

Millions of adults struggle with anxiety and overthinking, feeling trapped in a cycle of worry and stress. But it doesn't have to be this way. *"Healing Anxiety and Overthinking: Proven CBT Strategies for Lasting Relief"* offers a comprehensive guide to breaking free from the grip of anxiety using practical, proven **Cognitive Behavioral Therapy (CBT)** strategies.

❤ *Imagine waking up every day with a clear mind, free from the constant barrage of anxious thoughts*

This book is your roadmap to achieving that transformation in just 15 steps. You'll learn to understand the nature of your anxiety, identify its triggers, and apply effective techniques to manage and overcome it.

Take Control of Your Mental Health

Don't let anxiety and overthinking rule your life. With *"Healing Anxiety and Overthinking,"* you'll gain the tools and confidence to achieve peace of mind and live the life you deserve.

Discover More by Artem Kudelia
Scan the QR code or click the link to access his author page and full collection. Each book provides detailed insights and practical guidance, exemplifying his contributions to psychology and psychotherapy.